cejc
hist

Understanding
JORDAN
Today

JORDAN

Laura Perdew

Mitchell Lane
PUBLISHERS
P.O. Box 196
Hockessin, Delaware 19707

A Kid's Guide to
THE MIDDLE EAST

Irbid

Jarash
Jarash   Al Mafraq   Mahattat al Jufur

Al Balqa   Az Zarqa'   Mahattat al Haff

As Salt
Ma'daba   *'Amman
Queen Alia International Airport   Azraq ash Shishan

Jordan

Al Mazra'ah
Al Karak   Al Qatranah

As Safi

At Tafilah
Ba'ir

Ash Shawbak

Petra   Ma'an   Al Jafr

Ra's en Naqb

Al 'Aqabah

Al Mudawwara

TURKEY

SYRIA

LEBANON

IRAQ

PALESTINE

ISRAEL

JORDAN

AFGHANISTAN

IRAN

SAUDI
ARABIA

PUBLISHERS

Printing   1   2   3   4   5   6   7   8   9

Library of Congress Cataloging-in-Publication Data
Perdew, Laura.
 Understanding Jordan today / by Laura Perdew.
     pages cm. — (A kid's guide to the Middle East)
 Includes bibliographical references and index.
 ISBN 978-1-61228-654-9 (library bound)
 1. Jordan—Juvenile literature. I. Title.
 DS153.P47 2014
 956.95—dc23

                                                                2014020462

eBook ISBN: 9781612286778

PUBLISHER'S NOTE: The narrative used in portions of this book are an aid to comprehension. This narrative is based on the author's extensive research as to what actually occurs in a child's life in Jordan. It is subject to interpretation and might not be indicative of every child's life in Jordan. It is representative of some children and is based on research the author believes to be accurate. Documentation of such research is contained on pp. 60–61.

The Internet sites referenced herein were active as of the publication date. Due to the fleeting nature of some web sites, we cannot guarantee they will all be active when you are reading this book.

To reflect current usage, we have chosen to use the secular era designations BCE ("before the common era") and CE ("of the common era") instead of the traditional designations BC ("before Christ") and AD (*anno Domini,* "in the year of the Lord").

PBP

CONTENTS

BOLD words in text can be found in the glossary

Introduction

In the heart of the Middle East is the Hashemite Kingdom of Jordan. This country, more commonly known as Jordan, lies at the intersection of ancient trade routes. For many centuries, travelers through the region were met with open arms and refuge. This welcoming tradition continues in Jordan today. Visitors often receive numerous invitations for dinner or coffee. Jordanians are always willing to help and wanting to talk. And the nation itself is a safe haven for hundreds of thousands of refuges from other parts of the volatile region.

While its neighbors are regularly beset by violence, Jordan has remained stable. Since the country first became fully

The capital of Jordan, Amman, is a modern city with reminders of an ancient past. The Roman Temple of Hercules sits atop the hill and dates back to the second century CE.

independent in 1946, Jordan's kings have worked hard to maintain this peace. They have also sought peace for the region. And, they have worked to improve the lives of the people in Jordan. In addition, Jordan has relationships with nations around the world based on mutual respect.

Across the country, the people's daily lives are guided by many longstanding aspects of Arab culture. Yet Jordan is also a modern, progressive nation. Its citizens are fiercely proud of their country. And they are happy to share their vibrant culture and cuisine.

Students in Jordan, wearing their school uniforms, line up before entering the building.

CHAPTER 1
A Day in Jordan

Six o'clock on Sunday morning always comes too early for Noor. It is the first day of the school week. She spent Friday playing with friends. Saturday, as always, she'd gone to the weekly family lunch at her grandparents' house. They ate and talked for hours. Grandpa told stories to the kids. The cousins played together.

Her mother rubs her shoulder again. "Wake up, sleepy," she says. Noor drags herself out of bed. She puts on her school uniform pants, then a white button-down top. She goes to the kitchen for a quick bowl of cereal. Today she chooses Trix over Golden Grahams. Her father has already left for work. Her brother has left too, on his way to the high school he attends. Noor's mother sits with her in the kitchen until it is time for the school bus.

As the bus heads toward their private elementary school, one of Noor's friends pulls out her cell phone. The girls listen to music together. Most of the time they listen to modern Arab music, though sometimes Noor asks to change the station so she can listen to the older, more traditional music her mother loves. Noor can't wait until she gets a cell phone of her own. Luckily, her friend shares everything with Noor. "What's mine is yours!" they always say to each other.

They arrive at school by 8:00. Noor goes to the classroom where she'll spend the entire day with the same boys and girls. Different teachers come in to teach the different subjects. Today all the subjects are taught in English. Tomorrow their lessons will be conducted in Arabic. Noor loves her school and the

Jordanian students open textbooks and wait for their teacher's instructions.

community of students. Still, by 10:15 she can't concentrate on the science lesson. She is hungry again. Only 15 more minutes until breakfast.

At last it is 10:30. The students go to the cafeteria. Noor heads to her favorite spot—the sandwich line, where she orders the same thing almost every day. The man behind the counter holds up the bread. "*Labneh*, please," Noor says. She loves the sour-cream-like spread. "Then olive oil. And of course the **za'tar!** Maybe today, some salami, too, please." When the man is finished, he rolls up the sandwich and hands it to Noor. She finds a table with her friends.

Later in the day, after language arts and math, Noor and her classmates go out for recess. One of her favorite games is volleyball. Nearby, a group of boys plays basketball. If it is too hot, everyone lounges in the shade by the school building.

The school day is over at 3:00. Lunch at home is served at 3:30. As always, Noor's whole family is there. Today her mom has prepared Noor's favorite, *mansaf.* Yellow rice is piled on top of a piece of flatbread. Then lamb and roasted almonds are added. The lamb has cooked for a long time in *jameed*, a dried salted yogurt made from goat's milk that gives the meat its creamy, rich flavor.

Once the meal is finished, Noor asks her mom for one JD. JD is short for Jordanian dinar, which is similar to a dollar in the United States. It is enough money to buy candy at her favorite shop. Mom smiles and hands Noor the money. "But homework first," she says.

Noor has homework almost every day. She knows that finishing it comes before anything else. She wants to continue to do well in school. If she does, Noor may attend college, either in Jordan or in another country. Her oldest sister is already studying at a Canadian university.

When she finishes her homework, Noor straps on her roller blades. On the street she calls out to her neighbor friends. Soon a group of them are skating amongst the cars and traffic on their way to The Three Musketeers candy shop. The old man behind the counter smiles at the kids. He hands each of them a free piece of candy. Noor spends her money on her favorites, jelly beans and a lollipop. Noor's best friend buys Nerds. Another friend buys a Cadbury chocolate. After they eat their treats, the

IN CASE YOU WERE WONDERING

What are schools like in Jordan?
They are very much the same as schools in the United States. Students begin attending school at kindergarten and continue through high school. There are both public and private schools. Unlike in the US, however, it is the public schools that are religious. The private schools tend to be more liberal.

kids play in the streets until dusk. When the sun goes down, Noor goes home.

Around 8:00, Noor gets herself a quick dinner to eat in front of the TV. Then she turns on Cartoon Network. But she can't watch for long. Tomorrow is Monday, another school day. Soon

Jordanians have access to television shows from around the world, including cartoons from the United States.

it's time for bed. Noor falls asleep thinking of her sister. Noor wonders if she will be able to study in Canada, too. She's already visited her sister there once. She liked it very much. But going to school in London sounds good too. Or maybe even she could find a university in the United States.

AN OVERVIEW OF JORDAN

When you think of Jordan, what's the first thing that comes to your mind? Camels? Deserts? Men wearing a red and white headdress (called a **kaffiyeh**)? Jordan has all of these. And so much more.

The larger cities in Jordan, like the capital city of Amman, are very modern. Amman is a bustling city with high-rise buildings, buses, and cars. There are world-class hotels, many restaurants to choose from, nightclubs, and western stores, even Starbucks coffee shops! Yet Amman still has open markets in the older part of the city. Vendors there sell fresh fruits and vegetables and other items right on the sidewalk. People call out and sing in Arabic. Yet most everyone speaks English as well.

Above Amman is the Citadel, an ancient fortress. It contains Roman ruins which serve as a reminder of Jordan's rich past. This past is a history of many different conquering civilizations. Each left its mark. Their ruins are scattered across Jordan.

The landscape of Jordan is 90 percent desert.[2] Yet the rest of the land is amazingly diverse. Elevations range from below sea level at the Dead Sea, to more than 6,000 feet in the highlands. There are valleys, plateaus and **wadis**, or canyons. Many types of flora and fauna exist in Jordan, too. There are wildflowers, pine trees, desert grasses, and more. Lizards, the white oryx, wolves, and gulls are some of the many animals that call Jordan home.[3]

The King Abdullah I Mosque in Amman was built in the 1980s as a memorial to Jordan's first king.

The Bedouins (BED-oo-ins) in Jordan today live in much the same way their ancestors did hundreds of years ago. The word Bedouin comes from the Arabic word Bedu, which means "desert dweller."

CHAPTER 2
Deep Roots

To get to know Jordan, it is necessary to understand Jordan's location in the world. Basically Jordan is in the middle of the Middle East. Israel borders Jordan to the west. Its neighbor to the south and east is Saudi Arabia. To the north is Syria, while Iraq lies to the northeast. This central location made Jordan an important part of trade routes for many centuries. It also made Jordan a target for conquering armies. Today, though, Jordan is independent. And it continues to play a key role in the Middle East.

Jordan is home to some of the world's oldest civilizations. The first people to live there were **hunter-gatherers** during the Paleolithic Era, also called the Old Stone Age and dating back several hundred thousand years. These people hunted wild animals for meat and gathered wild plants. They were **nomadic**. That means they had no permanent home. Instead, they moved around depending on the seasons in search of food and water. This nomadic culture lies at the root of the ancient Bedouins, whose descendants still live in the deserts of Jordan today.[1]

By 8000 BCE people in the area began to plant and grow grains. They also **domesticated** animals. These developments provided reliable food sources and small settlements began to appear.

Between 8000 and 4500 BCE, the inhabitants of the region thrived in villages. People learned how to create channels to move water and how to store it. They found new food to harvest, such as lentils, cereal grains, and peas. During this era people began herding goats. They also learned how to use clay to make pottery, especially pots, bowls, and pitchers that could be used in everyday life. Jordan became a trade center. As trade and commerce grew, people created more trade routes. On each of these routes, additional settlements developed.[2]

By 3200 BCE, **city-states** had begun to emerge. These were individual cities with their own governments that controlled the land surrounding the city. Most city-states were in the northern part of the region. Nomadic Bedouin tribes continued to live in the southern part. For a time the area fell under Egyptian control. Under Egyptian rule things were peaceful and prosperous. Then, shortly before the end of the second millennium BCE the lands of Jordan began to experience regular invasions. Conquering empires included the Israelites, Assyrians, Babylonians, Persians, and Greeks. In 63 BCE the Romans conquered the region and built a number of great cities. One of the most notable is Jerash, north of Amman, where many ruins are still visible today. The Romans built roads to link key trading cities. Watchtowers were erected along the routes to protect traders.

The Roman emperor Theodosius made Christianity the official religion of Rome in the latter part of the fourth century CE. Jordan may have played a key role in its development and even its very survival during its early days. As the *Lonely Planet: Jordan* guidebook notes, "in 2008, 40 km (25 miles) northeast of Amman, archaeologists uncovered what they believe to be

IN CASE YOU WERE WONDERING

What is Amman named for?
Its name comes from "Rabbath Ammon," or "Great City of the Ammonites." The Ammonites were people who settled in the region about 1200 BCE.

the first church in the world. . . . These first Christians fled persecution in Jerusalem [by the Romans] and lived in secrecy, practicing their religion in the underground church."[3]

Eventually the Roman Empire split into eastern and western halves. Jordan lay in the eastern half, known as the Byzantine Empire, and became even more prosperous. This prosperity is evident in many of the churches, chapels, and other structures that were built during this time. Many of them were elaborately decorated with mosaics, which are detailed images made of tiles which depict people, animals, and even maps. Many of these mosaics have survived and may be seen at some of Jordan's historic sites.

Early in the seventh century the religion of **Islam** emerged in the Arabian Peninsula. Its followers, known as **Muslims**, quickly spread the new faith. Muslim armies defeated the Byzantines in 636 at the Battle of Yarmouk and assumed control of the region. Arabic became the official language. This period laid the foundation for the culture in Jordan that exists today.[4]

During the following centuries, several Muslim dynasties— the Umayyads, the Abbasids, the Fatimids, and the Ayyubids— controlled Jordan and the surrounding area. In 1250, still another Muslim dynasty, the Mamluks, overthrew the Ayyubids. In turn, the Mamluks were defeated by the Ottoman Turks in 1516. Ottoman rule continued for the next 400 years. For Jordan, Ottoman rule was a time of **oppression** and neglect. The Ottomans didn't care much about the people in the region. The population declined. Many villages were abandoned. Agriculture suffered. The only group that continued to do well was the Bedouins. These nomads in the desert continued to live as they had for centuries.

By the early 1900s, Arabs across the region were tired of Ottoman rule. The outbreak of World War I in 1914 gave them an opportunity to rid themselves of the Ottomans. During the conflict, the Ottomans sided with the Central Powers, primarily Germany and Austria-Hungary. They opposed the Allies, led by Great Britain and France. The Middle East was one of the most important theaters of the war. Seeking an advantage over the Ottomans, the British promised to support a unified Arab state when the war was over in exchange for Arab support during the fighting.

So in June 1916, the Arabs launched the Great Arab Revolt under the leadership of Hussein bin Ali, the head of the Hashemite family. "His objective in undertaking the Great Arab Revolt was to establish a single independent and unified Arab state stretching from Aleppo (Syria) to Aden (Yemen), based on the ancient traditions and culture of the Arab people, the upholding of Islamic ideals and the full protection and inclusion of ethnic religious minorities,"[5] notes an official Jordanian website. Hussein's sons Faisal and Abdullah led Arab armies, which used the desert for strategic attacks. Slowly Ottoman rule weakened through a combination of British and Arab assaults. The Ottomans were finally defeated in October, 1918.

But when the war was over, the British and French broke their promise of supporting an independent Arab state. Instead, they divided up the Middle East between themselves. France took control of modern-day Syria and Lebanon. The British portion was what is now Iraq and Palestine, which included the lands that later would become Jordan and Israel.

In 1921, the British named Abdullah as emir (which means "prince" or "commander") of the land that lay east of the Jordan River, though they remained in overall control. This land was called Transjordan, which means "across the Jordan River." As historian Richard Cavendish notes, "Afterwards Abdullah tried to persuade the British government to give him Palestine. He

Colonel Lawrence (second from left), also known as Lawrence of Arabia, stands on an airfield in Amman with Sir Herbert Samuel (to Lawrence's left), the British commissioner in Palestine, and Emir Abdullah (far right).

Mr. and Mrs. Winston Churchill (on the right) attend a reception at the Government House in Palestine on March 28, 1921. Sir Herbert Samuel is on Churchill's right and Emir Abdullah is next to Samuel.

had to settle for Transjordan, but his appetite for the Arab territory west of the Jordan remained."[6] Nearly 30 years later, his appetite would be satisfied. In the meantime, becoming Emir of Transjordan was the start of Abdullah's dream of creating a free Arab state.[7]

IN CASE YOU WERE WONDERING

What did the ancient people of Jordan use to build their homes?
Many used bricks made of sun-dried mud, while others used stone. For the roofs, they used wood, reeds and mud.

JERASH

The city of Jerash has been occupied continuously for more than 6,500 years. Perhaps the most notable part of its history began in 63 BCE, when it came under Roman control. During that time Jerash experienced significant growth as the Romans created a thriving urban center. They built paved roads lined with **colonnades**. On hilltops they erected grand temples. The Romans also constructed theatres, baths, and fountains. The city center contained open squares and plazas. The city was surrounded by a wall with towers and gates.

Today, the well-preserved ruins are among the world's most notable. One of the main attractions is the Hippodrome, which held about 15,000 spectators for sporting events such as chariot races. Up to ten chariots competed at the same time, doing several laps of the arena. The chariot races have been brought back to Jerash for modern visitors. The races are choreographed to look like they did hundreds of years ago, with trumpets, official battledresses, swords, and gladiators.

The annual Jerash Festival brings the ancient city to life every summer. It includes folk dancing, ballet, musical groups, and plays in the ancient theatres. In addition to performing arts, visitors can browse through a wide selection of traditional crafts.

The Roman amphitheater in Jerash is the site of both ancient and modern events.

Abdullah I was Jordan's first king. He dedicated his life to securing Jordan's independence and leading his nation.

CHAPTER 3
On Its Own—At Last!

Abdullah's first step was to set up a central government in Amman. At that time Amman was a small town with barely 3,000 people, some of whom lived in tents and even caves. Two years later the British recognized Transjordan as a state under its protection. In 1928 Abdullah established the country's first constitution.

Over the next several years, Abdullah won more control over Transjordan in a series of treaties with Britain. Then, at last, on March 22, 1946, the country became fully independent. Two months later Abdullah was proclaimed as king. The new country took the official name of the Hashemite Kingdom of Jordan.

The kingdom was soon involved in a major conflict. When the British had said they would support an Arab state during World War I, they also promised the Jews a homeland in Palestine. Because a movement called **Zionism**—the desire for a Jewish state in Palestine—had originated late in the nineteenth century, some Jews had already moved there. Their numbers increased during the following years. Because millions of Jews had perished in German gas chambers during World War II, support for a Jewish state increased when the conflict ended. Late in 1947, the newly established United Nations voted to partition, or divide, Palestine into two states: one Jewish, the other Arab.

Conflict between Jews and Arabs began right away. Jews believed they were regaining the homeland of their ancestors. Yet Arabs had lived there for centuries. In May, 1948, the Jewish State of Israel was officially formed. Jordan and four other Arab nations immediately attacked the new nation. But they didn't coordinate their attacks. The Israelis, on the other hand, were well-organized and defeated the invaders. An **armistice** in mid-1949 ended the fighting, but no formal peace treaty was signed. Tensions between Israel and Arab nations stayed high.

Jordanian troops had been by far the most effective Arab force during the conflict. They had taken control of what was called the West Bank area, which was part of the territory the United Nations had designated for the Palestinian Arab state, and defeated Israeli efforts to dislodge them. This resulted in one of the key developments in modern Middle East history. As an official Jordanian website notes, "Many Palestinian Arabs from the Jordanian-controlled areas found that union with Jordan was of vital importance to the preservation of Arab control over the 'West Bank' territories which had not fallen to the Israelis. Consequently, in December 1948, a group of Palestinian leaders and notables from the West Bank convened a historic conference in Jericho, where they called for King Abdullah to take immediate steps to unite the two banks of the Jordan into a single state under his leadership."[1]

In 1950, Jordan formally made the West Bank a part of Jordan. Only two governments—Great Britain and Pakistan—approved of the move. The Arab League, an organization consisting of several independent Arab states, largely disapproved.[2] The annexation meant that the Palestinians couldn't have their own state. But Abdullah moved forward. Arabs in the West Bank became Jordanian citizens. The country's population tripled. The prewar population of more than 400,000 was joined by half a million people in the West Bank and another half-million refugees from other parts of Palestine.

King Abdullah was assassinated on July 20, 1951 by a Palestinian who believed that he was going to sign a peace treaty with Israel. His eldest son Talal took the throne but had to give it up after only a short time. Talal's oldest son Hussein became king on May 2, 1953.

Jordan faced significant challenges due to the continuing presence of Palestinian refugees. Many of them hoped that their stay in Jordan was temporary and wanted to reclaim their homeland within Israel. To achieve this goal, they established the Palestinian Liberation Organization (PLO) in 1964 and soon began launching attacks on Israeli positions from bases in Jordan.

Three years later Israel won a decisive victory over Egypt, Syria, and Jordan in the Six-day War. They seized control of the entire West Bank. That set off another wave of refugees to Jordan.

In response, the PLO stepped up its attacks on Israel. The organization also began exerting more authority inside Jordan. PLO leader Yassir Arafat called for the overthrow of King Hussein's government. In September, 1970, the situation came to a head and Hussein ordered his armed forces to attack the PLO. Hussein's troops expelled the PLO from Jordan, forcing them to set up bases elsewhere. The PLO referred to their defeat as "Black September."[3]

In 1998, Jordan formally gave up any claim to the West Bank. Six years later the country signed a peace treaty with Israel. It was only the second Arab nation to so, following Egypt

IN CASE YOU WERE WONDERING

Why did King Talal only reign for 2 years?
He gave up the throne due to health reasons. His son, Hussein, did not take the throne right away, though. He had to wait almost a year, until he turned 18!

Troops surround a Jordanian tank during "Black September" fighting against the PLO. The tank is "hull down," giving it added protection from enemy fire.

in 1979. The treaty also established a relationship between Jordan and Israel to work together for trade, energy, and more.[4]

The Middle East continues to be unstable. Jordan, however, is relatively safe. In fact, it is often called "an oasis of stability in a troubled region."[5] This is the legacy of King Hussein. During his long rule (1953–1999) he worked to create unity in the Middle East. He wanted peace, both in that region and globally. He helped to build Jordan into the modern nation it is today. And he worked hard to improve the lives of the people of Jordan.

King Hussein I ruled Jordan from 1953 until his death in 1999. He successfully and peacefully led his country through the Cold War and four decades of Arab-Israeli conflicts.

HIS MAJESTY KING HUSSEIN I OF THE HASHEMITE KINGDOM OF JORDAN

Today, his son Abdullah II rules in the same spirit. As king, he is the country's leader. Yet in Jordan he must rule within the guidelines of a constitution. This type of government is a **constitutional monarchy**.

The first constitution in Jordan was written in 1928, before the country was even independent. Once the country gained its independence, the document was amended and officially adopted on November 28, 1947. During his short rule, King Talal made changes that held the government and its ministers more accountable. This is the document that governs Jordan today.[6]

Under the terms of the constitution, the government has three branches: executive, legislative, and judicial. The king has executive powers. That means he has the main responsibility for running the country. He appoints a prime minister who oversees the daily operations of the government. The king appoints a cabinet as well, to assist the prime minister.

The legislative branch is called the National Assembly and has two houses. The Senate, or House of Notables, has 60 members appointed by the king. The Chamber of Deputies has 160 members elected by the people to four-year terms. Nearly 40 seats are reserved specifically for women, Christians, Bedouins, and Chechens and/or Circassians.[7]

The judicial branch is independent from the others. The highest court is the seven-member Supreme Court. The king appoints the chief justice and approves the others, who are selected by a panel known as the Higher Judicial Council.[8]

While Jordan is not a full democracy like the United States, it is one of the most democratic countries in the region. However, people still hope for certain reforms. For one, there is some corruption in the government. Citizens would also like a larger voice in government.

THE HASHEMITES

The Hashemites trace their ancestry to Hashim ibn Abd Manaf, who lived in the Arabian city of Mecca during the late fifth and early sixth centuries. Many historians believe that he was the great-grandfather of the Prophet Muhammad, the founder of Islam. Starting in 1201, a Hashemite was always the Sharif of Mecca. That meant he was responsible for the administration of the cities of Mecca and Medina, the two holiest sites in the religion of Islam.

The last Sharif was Hussein bin Ali. He began the Great Arab Revolt in 1916 in an effort to establish a free Arab state, though he was too old to take a direct role in the fighting. His son Abdullah finally won Jordan's independence in 1946 and ruled as King Abdullah I. Abdullah's grandson, Hussein, is known as the father of modern Jordan. He gave the country stability and led his country through the conflicts in the Middle East. King Hussein was well respected in Jordan and across the world.

Hussein's oldest son, Abdullah, took the throne as King Abdullah II on June 9, 1999 after the death of his father. He is married to Queen Rania, who works to promote social welfare in Jordan. They have four children. The oldest son, Prince Hussein, is the crown prince. One day he will become Jordan's king.

The Royal Family (from left): the king and queen's daughters, Iman and Salma; their oldest son, Crown Prince Hussein; Queen Rania; and King Abdullah II. The couple also has a fourth child, Prince Hashem.

Goat hair tents are designed to protect the Bedouin from heat and cold. During the dry, hot summers, many gaps and holes in the fabric allow air to move around and the tents stay cool. During the winter, the fabric shrinks and closes up the holes. The tents end up being warm and dry.

CHAPTER 4
The Face of a Nation

Jordan is an open and tolerant nation, which is somewhat uncommon in the Middle East. In Jordan, the cultural rights of all citizens are protected. People of any religion or ethnic group have guaranteed freedoms. Groups may teach and use their own languages. Religious and ethnic groups can create their own schools and clubs. Different places of worship are welcomed. This tradition of tolerance has helped Jordan to create unity among citizens. It has also helped the country to maintain stability within its borders.[1]

Today an estimated 6.5 million people live in Jordan. Nearly all of them are Muslims. Muslims believe that the Prophet Muhammad received the final message to humans from God. This word of God is contained in the **Qur'an**, the holy book of Islam. Most of the remaining population, about two percent, are Christians.

The vast majority of Jordanians are also Arabs. All the people with Arabian origins share a language, customs, and beliefs. This is where much of Jordan's culture comes from. Jordan also has small numbers of Circassians (a group of people who fled Russian expansion into their homeland in western Asia and made Jordan their home), Chechens, and Armenians.[2]

One of the largest groups of Arabs in Jordan are the Bedouin, who are often called the backbone of Jordan. For centuries, Bedouins were nomads. They had no permanent home. Instead they moved around to find food and water. They herded goats in the Jordanian desert. Bedouins use tents made from goat hair, called *beit al-sha'ar*, which literally means "house of hair." Other Bedouins lived in caves in the sandstone rock near the ancient ruins of Petra. Many Bedouin are goat herders. Camels are also extremely important to the Bedouin as a source of income and transport. The birth of a new "calf" is a treasured event. It is a symbol of the wealth of its owner.[3]

Bedouins are very welcoming and warm people. When guests arrive, coffee is offered right away as a form of welcome. The second cup of coffee honors the visitor. The third cup is simply for pleasure. As part of the Bedouin heritage, no traveler is ever turned away.

Some Bedouin are worried about losing their culture. Fewer young people are choosing to live like their ancestors as modern technology is seeping into their world.

Another important group of Arabs in Jordan are the Palestinians who fled to Jordan from their homeland when Israel was created in 1948. According to estimates, Palestinians make up more than half of the population of Jordan.[4]

Since the time the Palestinians first arrived, Jordan welcomed them and granted them full citizenship, the only nation in the Middle East to do that. In Jordan, Palestinians have the right to vote. They are represented in the government. And they are free to work and own businesses like all Jordanians.

Many Palestinians live and work in Jordan's towns and cities. But others remain in refugee camps. In some camps concrete buildings have replaced tents and services such as schools, food aid, and health care have been established. Yet while agencies try to improve conditions in camps, there are still many problems such as poor sewage systems, overcrowding, poverty, and high unemployment.

Even though the constitution guarantees them equal rights, some Palestinians believe that they are not quite equal. Jobs are often harder to come by. Good housing may not be as easy to find. Palestinians are not equally represented in the upper class. They hope that reforms will eventually bring full equality.[5]

Continuing turmoil in the Middle East has brought other refugees to Jordan. Refugees from Iraq began arriving in 2003 following the American-led invasion that overthrew the regime of the country's dictator Saddam Hussein. The Jordanian government estimates that about 450,000 Iraqis are now in the

Jordanians, Palestinians, and Iraqis take part in an anti-war protest in Amman on March 30, 2003. Around the world people took to the streets of their cities to protest the US-led war on Iraq, which began on March 20.

Women watch a tent being erected as other Syrian refugees go about their daily business in a refugee camp in Za'atari, Jordan. Record numbers of refugees fled the violence and bombings in Syria to the safety of Jordan. Their numbers, however, have overwhelmed the refugee camps.

country. Most are unable to obtain legal status in Jordan, and returning to their former homes is out of the question.[6]

Hundreds of thousands of Syrians also fled to Jordan for safety following the outbreak of civil war in their country in 2011. The new refugees not only add to overcrowding, but also compete for jobs and are willing to work for lower wages. Hospitals are overloaded. And water continues to be scarce.

The daily arrival of new refugees is pushing Jordan to its limits. When Transjordan was formed in 1921, the population was about 200,000. Today there are at least 30 times as many people in the country. Accommodating all of them is a major challenge. Jordan wants to continue offering refuge. Yet it must find ways to deal with the increasing strain on resources from so many people.

WATER SHORTAGE

One of the greatest challenges facing Jordan is a shortage of water. The demand for water in Jordan is greater than the supply. This is not a new problem in this arid land, as Jordan is the Earth's fourth-driest country. The annual rainfall is less than 12 inches (300 millimeters) annually. In some parts of Jordan people rely on water trucks. While the water from these trucks is expensive, they cannot do without it.

One problem is that neighboring countries have diverted water that Jordan relies on. As newspaper editor Ayman al-Safadi observes, "Syria has built hundreds of dams on the river flow in the Syrian territory, and it has not honored agreements that it has signed with Jordan, and the result has been that, for many, many years now, Syria has been stealing tremendous amounts of water that legally belongs to Jordan."[7]

Another issue making the water problem worse is population increase. Much of this increase is due to the influx of refugees from Palestine that began about 70 years ago, and aggravated by more recent events in Iraq and Syria.

In addition, Jordan's agri-culture industry consumes more than half the country's water supply. The distribution of water for irrigation must be carefully planned. Still, the amount of water available in Jordan is expected to continue declining. Farmers are very worried.

Since water is so scarce in Jordan, many people have to rely on storage tanks to get water.

Jordan has had help from the United States and other countries. In June 2007 the US gave Jordan $45 million dollars to help the country manage its water supply. Jordan's peace treaty with Israel is also helpful. The country is developing pipelines, dams and treatment facilities to bring water from Israel. More dams on the Yarmouk and Jordan Rivers are planned too. This will allow Jordan to collect and store more floodwater during the rainy season.

A man sells Arabic coffee to tourists near the Ajloun Castle in northern Jordan.

CHAPTER 5
Social Jordan

"*Ahlan wa salhlan!*" is a common phrase in Jordan. It means "Welcome!" Jordanians are social and warm people. Family and friends always take care of one another. Jordanians are kind to outsiders and strangers as well. They frequently extend invitations for tea or coffee. Coffee is an important part of socializing. Friends meet at coffee houses to share news and gossip. Traditional coffee houses in Jordan are for men only, while modern coffee shops—especially in urban areas—provide places where both men and women socialize.[1]

Food is also an important element of Jordanian culture. The cuisine has an Arab style that is part of the country's heritage.

Breakfast is generally eaten much later than in America. For example, in schools breakfast may not be served until around 10:00. Lunch is customarily served at home in mid-afternoon. Dinner is eaten late, usually around 8:00 pm. Many times, meals last for hours. People talk and eat, then talk some more.[2]

Some of the staples of Jordanian cooking are grains, cheese, and yogurt. Dried and fresh fruits and vegetables are key ingredients in most recipes. The national dish of Jordan is *mansaf*. It is made of lamb cooked in *jameed*, then spooned over rice piled on a piece of flatbread. Sometimes nuts are sprinkled on top. People are very serious about their *mansaf* and take a long time to prepare it.

Jordanians enjoy sweets too. One favorite is *knafeh*. This traditional dessert is made of sweet flaky pastry with soft cheese inside. After it is baked, a sugary syrup is drizzled over it.

knafeh

Food in Jordan provides more than nutrition. It is a key part of social customs. There are many occasions in Jordan to gather and feast.

Because nearly all Jordanians are Muslims, the holy month of Ramadan is observed nationwide. It is when Muhammad received the message of God. Ramadan is a time of spiritual cleansing.[3] During Ramadan, Muslims cannot eat or drink during daylight hours. At dusk each day people begin celebrating. Celebrations include gathering with family and friends, music, and lots of food. The end of Ramadan is marked by **Eid al-Fitr**, a three-day festival. There is more eating and gathering with family.

Weddings provide one of the favorite occasions for celebrations. Jordanians typically marry in their early-to-mid-20s. Often two people will meet, fall in love, and then marry with the approval of their families. Yet there are still some arranged marriages in Jordan, which usually take the form of an "introduction." The families of the man and woman set up a meeting when the two young people meet for the first time. After this meeting they decide if they want to marry.[4]

A wedding in Jordan is a grand affair that ends up being one of the biggest expenses in a Jordanian man's life. He is responsible for all the costs, including the honeymoon! On the day of the wedding, a **zaffeh**—a group of professional dancers and singers—goes to the groom's house where they play music, clap, sing, and dance. They take him to his bride's house, then escort the couple to the wedding and perform all along the way. After the ceremony, there is a small reception for family.

IN CASE YOU WERE WONDERING

What are wedding dresses like in Jordan?

In the modern areas of Jordan, women wear white gowns, much like in other parts of the world. More conservative Muslim women wear veils that cover part or all of their face. And in the Bedouin culture, brides wear colorful handmade dresses with intricate embroidery.

Then the big party starts. Sometimes there are 600-700 guests! Music, both Arabic and English, is played and guests dance the **dabke**, a traditional folk dance that is common across the Middle East. Men and women join hands. They dance in a semicircle, stomping their feet. Then there is a huge feast late in the evening followed by more dancing. Often the party lasts until the early hours of the following day![5]

Deaths also bring people together during a traditional three-day mourning period. The family of the deceased arranges a big gathering place. Friends and family come to pay their respects to the family. Everyone who knew the deceased is expected to attend. Even enemies visit to show respect. Traditionally the family provides food for all guests, though sweets are not served.[6]

This respect Jordanians show one another is an important part of their culture. Jordanians are honest and courteous as well. Overall, relationships are very important. When visitors to Jordan are invited for coffee or a meal, the invitation is genuine. Jordanians greet everyone like an old friend. There is much handshaking. Jordanians are likely to stop one another on the street to ask advice, even if they don't know each other. Old friends greet each other with a long series of cheek-kisses. This is followed by backslapping and an exchange of inquiries into one's well-being. Truly, Jordanians are so social, it is almost impossible to be alone!

IN CASE YOU WERE WONDERING

How are children treated in Jordan?
Children are extremely important, and most families have more than three children.[7]

THE AMMAN MESSAGE

After the September 11, 2001 terrorist attacks in the United States, many people around the world feared and disliked Muslims. Muslims themselves even questioned the **extremist** position of the attackers. In response to this, King Abdullah II asked for help from Muslim leaders throughout the world. He wanted to define the principles of Islam to his fellow Muslims and the rest of the world. As a Hashemite, Abdullah felt responsible for upholding and defending the Islamic faith. That is what his family had done for hundreds of years.

King Abdullah II addresses the General Assembly at the United Nations in New York City.

During Ramadan in 2004, King Abdullah published the Amman Message. It defines what Islam is, and what it is not, as stated in the Qur'an. The message is also clear about the actions that truly represent Islam. It describes the values of Islam, including tolerance and moderation. According to the Amman Message, the principles of Islam include:

Honoring all people, regardless of race or religion

Speaking with kindness and respect

Showing mercy for all

Treating others the way they wish to be treated

Respecting human life

Practicing tolerance, forgiveness, and justice

The message rejects extremism. In fact, it specifically criticizes the use of violence in the name of Islam. Through this message, Abdullah tried to lessen the world's fear and hatred of Islam and to promote understanding. His goal was to see respect among different faiths, cultures, and nations. Ultimately this respect leads to peaceful relations, a common theme in the work of his father, King Hussein.[8]

An artist makes sand art at a tourist shop that sells handmade sand paintings in bottles.

CHAPTER 6
Past Meets Present in the Arts

Jordan's rich history is reflected in its art, dance, and music. Crafts originating thousands of years ago remain an important part of Jordan's culture. These crafts are also important to Jordan's economy. Artisans sell their work in open markets in towns and cities across Jordan.

It's likely that ceramics is the oldest form of arts and crafts in Jordan. It may have begun by accident. Historians believe that more than 8,000 years ago, someone in the Middle East dropped a lump of clay into a fire. When the fire cooled, the person realized that the clay had hardened—which must have been amazing![1] This discovery spread rapidly, and people began shaping the clay to suit their needs. They made platters, bowls, and other similar items for use in everyday life. Modern Jordanian pottery has evolved from these roots into a true art form, featuring bright colors and designs.

Weaving began as a necessity too. Bedouin women wove rugs, cushions, tents, and other useful items on a loom using goat hair and sheep wool. They used natural dyes for the red, dark blue, green, orange and black colors in patterns of stripes and diamonds that characterized their output. The art started to die out when Bedouins began to settle in established communities. Artisans and international organizations came together to save the craft and create a source of income for both rural and urban women. Jewelry is another traditional Bedouin craft; Bedouins typically make their jewelry out of silver, glass beads, and stones.

Dating back more than 2,000 years, glassblowing is another long-established Jordanian craft. A much more recent glass craft involves pouring sand into bottles to create intricate designs. There are more than twenty different colors of sand in Jordan, so the artists can achieve great detail in their images with careful placement of the sand. "The bottles are inexpensive, and their playful patterns are unique to Jordan," notes the Jordanian Embassy website. "Some Jordanians learn this craft as a child, including collecting the necessary materials from the mountains and caves of Jordan."[2]

Music is another important art form. Traditional Arab songs tell stories. The singing is accompanied by instruments such as a *nay*, an *oud*, or a *tableh*. A *nay* is a type of flute. An *oud* is a stringed pear-shaped wooden instrument. And the *tableh* is a hand drum used to keep rhythms. The traditional music, which

A Jordanian man plays an oud inside a tent in Wadi Rum.

is often like poetry, is still very much a part of Jordanian culture. Yet new music is also popular. There are now modern Arab music artists. Young people also enjoy Western artists and other music of all kinds, and like to listen to it on their phones and iPods.

The week-long Al Balad Music Festival, held every summer in Amman, promotes music from across the Arab world. It also encourages the exchange of music among Arabs. Written literature in Jordan is relatively new. In the past, Arab literature was entirely oral.

In fact, the Bedouin have a rich tradition of storytelling, with stories passed down from one generation to the next. As more Bedouin settle in villages, writers have begun to transcribe the ancient stories and thereby preserve their heritage for future generations.[3]

Modern literature in Jordan deals with issues facing the country. It also includes common themes from the past such as love, honor, and war and displays the range of religious, political and literary beliefs.

Author Fadia Faqir is a voice for Arab women. While Jordan is more **progressive** than other Middle Eastern countries, women still face many issues being female in the Arab world. Perhaps their biggest challenge is finding their place in a **patriarchal** society. Faqir had first-hand experience with this challenge. Her father refused to allow her to travel to England to study writing even though she was well into her 20s. Although he eventually relented, it took many years for them to finally reconcile.[4]

Another modern Jordanian author is Elias Farkouh, who explores how different cultures, religions, and politics have shaped the Middle East. He also shows how these conditions have affected the people. A third notable author, Jamal Naji, was born in a refugee camp. His work deals with the Palestinian experience.

Jordan also has a thriving children's literature industry. Some books have the same themes as American books, though often with a particularly Jordanian slant. For example, in *Uncle Khalfan's Sheep*, the title character bundles his sheep into his truck and drives them to the dentist. "The story helps the child deal with his/her feelings of fear from the dentist and talk about them through the characters of the story,"[5] notes the publisher's website. Many books touch on religion and traditions. *Why Not?* examines villagers' reactions when a girl replaces her father in the traditionally male task of waking them for Suhoor, the pre-dawn meal during Ramadan.[6] Still other titles look at what happens when the old and new intersect.

The mix of old and new is what makes Jordan such a unique place. Old traditions, customs, and arts are everywhere. They are very much a part of everyday life and guide how people interact. Yet Jordan is also a modern nation in which many Bedouin drive trucks instead of camels and young people have access to the same technology as young people in America. Somehow, old and new meet graciously in Jordan. It results in a modern culture with a foundation in the past.

IN CASE YOU WERE WONDERING

Are there movies in Jordan?

Jordan has a small movie industry. However, a number of famous movies have been filmed there, such as *Lawrence of Arabia* (1962). Another is *Indiana Jones and the Last Crusade* (1989), which includes a scene filmed at *Petra*. A third is *The Hurt Locker* (2008), which won the Academy Award for Best Picture.

PETRA

Hidden among looming walls of sandstone in the Jordanian desert is a city carved out of stone. For hundreds of years Petra was a well-kept secret. The only people who knew of its existence were the Bedouins. It wasn't until 1812 that the "Lost City" was rediscovered by the Western world. Today it is Jordan's most-visited tourist destination.

Access is through a long, narrow gorge. On either side are looming walls of red sandstone hundreds of feet high. Then the passage opens, revealing the face of the Treasury. The face of the building is all that can be seen. The rest is built into the rock.

The city was built by a group of people called the Nabateans. Little is known about them. Some believe they are the ancestors of the Bedouins today. They constructed Petra about 2,300 years ago and it soon became highly prosperous.

The Treasury building in Petra

That's because it lay along the Silk Road, an important trade route connecting China to Europe, the Arab world, and other destinations. The Chinese traded their prized silk for a variety of products. Petra offered a place of refuge from the unforgiving desert sun for trading caravans. It was also a place to get water. The Nabateans were skilled at water storage and conservation, using a system of dams and canals. Archaeologists have discovered secret passageways leading to storage facilities underground.

Utilizing a mix of Syrian, Greek, and Egyptian styles, architects created temples, tombs, and passageways. The city also featured colonnaded streets, an amphitheater, and a monastery.

For centuries Petra was wealthy and powerful. Yet around the second or third centuries CE, trade routes changed. Travelers no longer stopped in Petra. The city gradually lost its importance. By the seventh century, it was completely deserted.

A Bedouin man, wearing a *kaffiyah*, kneels for the Salat, the practice of formal worship in Islam. Salat is usually done five times a day.

CHAPTER 7
Ancient Land, Modern Attitude

Since Jordan is a progressive nation with deep roots in the past, it has been called the "ancient land with a modern attitude."[1] Amman, Jordan's capital, is a modern metropolis. The city has high-rise buildings, classy hotels, dance clubs, trendy restaurants, and high-tech companies. Yet alongside newer buildings are traditional shops and open marketplaces. Artisans sell crafts that have been part of Jordanian culture for centuries. Just outside the city, shepherds tend their goats as they have always done.

The mix of old and new is apparent in how people dress. Many Jordanians are quite fashionable, dressing in much the same way as people in Europe or the United States. Yet walking next to them may be a woman wearing a **hijab** to cover her head and hair. More conservative Muslim women may wear a long dress that covers almost their entire body.[2]

Among the Bedouins, the traditional clothing is long, loose fitting gowns for both men and women. This keeps them cool in the summer. In the winter, they add layers for warmth. Most Bedouin men still wear a *kaffiyeh*, the traditional headdress. Originally these were worn to protect people from blowing sand or from the heat. The Bedouin also mix ancient traditions with modern technology. It is not unusual for Bedouin to transport a camel long distances in the back of a pick-up truck. And some young Bedouin have begun to use remote-control jockeys for camel races![3]

Women in Jordan today have many freedoms. They can vote, drive, and participate in business and government. Since

Camel races in the desert remain an important part of Bedouin culture.

1994 the Directorate of Women's Affairs has worked to improve the role of women. One woman in particular has helped to improve women's rights in everyday life. She is Princess Aisha, King Hussein's daughter, who serves as a lieutenant colonel in the Jordanian Army.

The royal family has brought about reforms in other ways. After taking office, Abdullah II amended the constitution to increase the role of citizens in politics. The king, along with his wife, Queen Rania, has implemented education reforms too. Jordan has invested more money in education than many other nations in the Middle East. The king and queen believe that education is the right of every child, both boys and girls.

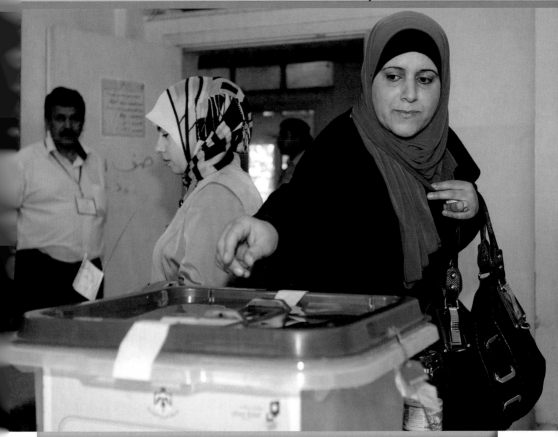

A Jordanian woman casts her ballot for municipal elections at a polling station in Amman on August 27, 2013.

Education will benefit the economy as well. According to Queen Rania, "Paying for education makes people more prosperous. For every $1 spent on education, a further $10–$15 is generated as a result of higher growth."[5]

Economic development in Jordan has been an ongoing challenge. The country has very few natural resources. Even though many people believe that every nation in the Middle East has abundant amounts of oil, this is not true of Jordan. As a result, the majority of Jordan's money comes from services, including tourism. The nation's main exports are clothes, fertilizer and medicines.[6] Even so, Jordan relies heavily on foreign aid. Many people live in poverty. Unemployment is high.

Since taking the throne, King Abdullah has tried to change this situation by creating jobs and growing the economy. As one step, he has **privatized** government-owned companies. That means he has allowed private companies to buy many formerly government-run businesses. He has also encouraged companies from other countries to start businesses in Jordan.

Jordan is dedicated to preserving its wild places too. In the past, population growth and pollution have harmed the environment. Many animals became endangered. To change this, the country began to think about wildlife preservation and environmental issues. In 1966, Jordan was the first country in the Middle East to set up a non-government organization to guide preservation. Today the Royal Society for the Conservation of Nature (RSCN) has the responsibility to protect Jordan's natural heritage. It has established numerous protected areas in Jordan and promotes public education and awareness of environmental issues.

Despite these challenges, Jordan holds a solid position in the Middle East. King Abdullah respects his country's Arab heritage, yet stays committed to relationships with nations around the globe. He believes that his country can be a role model for the rest of the region.

IN CASE YOU WERE WONDERING

What is the literacy rate in Jordan?
Nearly 96 percent of Jordanians aged 15 and over can read and write.[7]

UNIQUE GEOGRAPHICAL FEATURES

Despite its relatively small size, Jordan has several unique geographic features. Perhaps the best-known is the Dead Sea. It lies in the Jordan Valley, on the western border of Jordan. It is the lowest point on earth, at 1,312 feet (400 meters) below sea level. What draws people to the Dead Sea are its extremely salty, warm, healing waters which can be up to 10 times saltier than the ocean! Because of this, it is easy to lie back and float on the surface. This high salt content prevents plants and animals from living there and accounts for its name.

The town of Aqaba provides Jordan's only access to the ocean. It is at the southernmost part of Jordan, on the Red Sea. Its key location has played an important role in trade routes for centuries. Tourists love its warm, sandy beaches and clear waters with a wide variety of coral and marine life. In fact, there are over 1,000 different fish species in the Gulf of Aqaba. People enjoy snorkeling and scuba diving among sea turtles, brightly colored fish, and dolphins.

Just northeast of Aqaba is Wadi Rum, where sandstone rocks rise more than 5,000 feet (1,500 meters) above the earth. There are vast expanses of desert, canyons to explore, and hidden water holes. This geographic marvel is still home to many Bedouin tribes.

Jordan has wetlands, too! East of Amman, in the desert, Azraq is a wetland oasis as a result of its seasonal rains that create pools and marshes for migrating birds. Today it is a nature reserve and the home to 2,000 kinds of wildflowers.

Aqaba, on the shores of the Red Sea, is an important city in Jordan for trade and tourism.

MUJADARRA

Lentils have been harvested in Jordan for thousands of years. Combined with rice and onions, they make a simple vegetarian dish called mujadarra. Allow about 45 minutes to make it. Be sure to ask **an adult** for help in slicing the onions and using the stove!

Ingredients

5 onions
3 tablespoons olive oil
1 cup green lentils
4¼ cups water
1 cup uncooked
  white rice
½ teaspoon cinnamon
½ teaspoon allspice
¼ teaspoon black
  pepper
3 tablespoons salt
1 cup plain Greek yogurt

Instructions

1. Slice onions and sauté in 3 tablespoons olive oil over medium heat until soft and brown. Be patient. This takes a while.
2. While the onions cook, bring water and lentils to a boil in a pot (3-quart or larger). Once the lentils boil, reduce heat to low, cover, and simmer for 15 minutes.
3. Add about two-thirds of the cooked onions to the lentils. Reserve the remaining one-third as a topping.
4. Add cinnamon and allspice to lentils and stir. Add uncooked rice. Bring to a boil again. Cover and simmer for 15 minutes, or until rice is tender.
5. Add salt and pepper.
6. To serve, spoon the mujadarra onto individual plates. Top with leftover sautéed onions and a dollop of yogurt.

JORDAN  CRAFT

CLAY

Making items out of clay originated thousands of years ago in the region that is now Jordan. At first, people made vessels to use in everyday life. Pottery remains an important craft in modern Jordan.

Materials

Air-dry clay (available in most craft stores)
Rolling pin
Plastic knives and forks
Cookie cutters (optional)
Bowl of water
Rag (for cleaning your fingers)

Instructions

What you make is limited only by your imagination. Here are a few ideas:

1. Pinch pot—form the clay into a smooth ball. Press your thumbs into the center of the ball. Slowly pinch and turn the clay to form and thin the sides of the pot. Shape however you wish!
2. Animals—use different sizes and shapes of clay to create small figurines of any animal
3. Decorative piece—roll the clay out with the rolling pin until it is about ⅛ inch thick. Then use the cookie cutter to cut out a shape. Use the knife or fork to etch designs into the clay, or add pieces of clay in different shapes.
4. Cup—roll the clay out with the rolling pin until it is about ⅛ inch thick. Then use the knife to cut the edges. For a cup, first cut out a rectangle. Pick the rectangle slab up, and loop into the shape of a cup. Use your fingers and extra water to seal the edges of the clay together. Then place the cylinder on top of another slab of clay. Around the bottom of the cylinder, cut out a round piece to be the bottom of your cup. Again use your fingers and water to attach the edges of the clay. Use the knife and fork to etch designs or pictures into the side of your cup.

WHAT YOU SHOULD KNOW ABOUT JORDAN

Official country name: Hashemite Kingdom of Jordan
Official language: Arabic; English is widely understood
Capital: Amman
Ethnic groups: Arab 98%, others 2% (primarily Armenian, Chechen, and Circassian)
Religions: Muslim 97.2%, Christian 2.2%, others .6%
Area: 35,475 square miles (91,900 sq km), slightly smaller than Indiana
Population: 6.5 million
Largest cities: Amman (1,920,000), Zarqa (795,000), Irbid (308,000), Russeifa (270,000), Wadi Al Seer (185,000)
Highest point: Jabal Umm ad Dami, 6,083 feet (1,854 m)
Lowest point: Dead Sea, -1312 feet (-400 m)
Climate: In the northern and western parts of the country, summers are warm and dry. Winters are mild and wet. Sometimes snow falls in the northern highlands. Average temperatures range between 54° and 77° F (12°–25° C). Jordan's deserts are arid, getting less than 2 inches of rain (5 centimeters) a year. And in the summer, they get very hot, up to 115° F (46° C)!

FLAG: Jordan's flag was officially adopted in 1928. It is based on the banner of the Great Arab Revolt used during World War I. The black, white, and green bands represent different dynasties that previously ruled the region. The red triangle represents the Hashemite dynasty. The star in the center has seven points, which represent seven verses of Islamic belief at the beginning of the Qur'an.

TIMELINE

DATES BCE

c. 8000	People begin creating semi-permanent settlements.
c. 3200	City states begin to emerge, marking a time of increased civilization.
c. 300	The city of Petra is established.
63	Roman forces conquer the region.

DATES CE

106	Jordan becomes part of the Roman province of Arabia.
324	The Byzantine era begins and Christianity spreads through the Middle East.
636	Islamic armies invade and control Jordan.
1516	The Ottomans defeat the last of the Islamic armies, and rule the area for the next 400 years.
1916	The Great Arab Revolt begins in June in an attempt to free Arab lands from Ottoman rule and create a unified Arab state.
1918	Ottoman rule ends, but Arab territories are divided between Britain and France.
1921	Emir Abdullah establishes a central government in Transjordan.
1923	Britain officially recognizes Transjordan as a state but retains some control.
1946	Jordan becomes fully independent on March 22; Abdullah is crowned as king two months later and Jordan takes the official name, "The Hashemite Kingdom of Jordan."
1948	After the new nation of Israel is created, Jordan and other Arab nations attack Israel and refugees flock to Jordan.
1950	Jordan formally annexes the West Bank.
1951	King Abdullah is assassinated on July 20.
1953	Abdullah's grandson Hussein becomes king.
1966	Jordan becomes the first nation in the Middle East to begin preservation efforts with the establishment of the Royal Society for the Conservation of Nature.
1967	Israel regains the West Bank in the Six-Day War.
1970	"Black September" civil war breaks out in Jordan between Palestinian and Jordanian forces.
1988	Jordan gives up all claims to the West Bank.
1994	Jordan and Israel sign a peace treaty.
1999	King Abdullah II takes the throne on June 9.
2001	Jordan, Syria, and Egypt combine on a $300 million electricity project linking the three nations.
2003	Iraqi refugees begin fleeing to Jordan after US-led invasion of their country.
2004	King Abdullah II delivers the Amman Message, reasserting the true principles of Islam.
2011	The Syrian civil war begins, forcing hundreds of thousands of Syrians to take refuge in Jordan.
2014	World Health Organization announces that nearly 600,000 Syrian refugees are in Jordan.

CHAPTER NOTES

Chapter 1—A Day in Jordan

1. Sara Alamad (Colorado University student born and raised in Jordan), personal interview February 4, 2014.

2. Norbert Balit, *I Have Seen the Earth Change—Jordan* (An ADAMIS Production, 2010). http://www.youtube.com/watch?v=8QVuZ0TSoPE

3. "Wildlife and Vegetation," Hashemite Kingdom of Jordan. http://www.kinghussein.gov.jo/geo_env2.html

Chapter 2—Deep Roots

1. "History," The Embassy of the Hashemite Kingdom of Jordan. http://jordanembassyus.org/page/history

2. Ibid.

3. Jenny Walker and Matthew Firestone, *Lonely Planet: Jordan*. Seventh Edition (Oakland, CA: Lonely Planet, 2007), p. 42.

4. "The Islamic Periods and the Crusades," Hashemite Kingdom of Jordan. http://www.kinghussein.gov.jo/his_islam_crusades.html

5. "Sharif Hussein bin Ali." http://www.kinghussein.gov.jo/sharif_hussein.html

6. Richard Cavendish, "Jordan Formally Annexes the West Bank," *History Today*, April 2000. http://www.historytoday.com/richard-cavendish/jordan-formally-annexes-west-bank

7. "The Making of Transjordan," Hashemite Kingdom of Jordan. http://www.kinghussein.gov.jo/his_transjordan.html

Chapter 3—On Its Own—At Last!

1. "The Tragedy of Palestine," The Hashemite Kingdom of Jordan. http://www.kinghussein.gov.jo/his_palestine.html

2. Helen Chapin Metz, editor. *Jordan: A Country Study*. Washington, DC: GPO for the Library of Congress, 1989. http://countrystudies.us/jordan/10.htm

3. "1970: Civil War breaks out in Jordan," BBC News. http://news.bbc.co.uk/onthisday/hi/dates/stories/september/17/newsid_4575000/4575159.stm

4. Clyde Haberman, "Israel and Jordan Sign Peace Accord." *New York Times*, October 26, 1994. https://www.nytimes.com/learning/general/onthisday/big/1026.html#article

5. "Jordan Today," His Majesty King Abdullah II Ibn Al Hussein. http://kingabdullah.jo/index.php/en_US/pages/view/id/152.htmlhttp://kingabdullah.jo/index.php/en_US/pages/view/id/152.html

6. "The Constitution," Hashemite Kingdom of Jordan. http://www.kinghussein.gov.jo/government1.html#The Constitution

7. "Jordan," The CIA World Factbook. https://www.cia.gov/library/publications/the-world-factbook/geos/jo.html

8. Ibid.

Chapter 4—The Face of a Nation

1. "The People of Jordan," The Hashemite Kingdom of Jordan. http://www.kinghussein.gov.jo/people.html

2. Ibid.

3. *Living Cultures—The Last Bedu of Petra and Wadi Rum (Jordan)*, (ZED. ADEQUAT Limited, nd.) http://www.youtube.com/watch?v=hhz2nTu-PFA

4. Assessment for Palestinians in Jordan, Minorities at Risk. http://www.cidcm.umd.edu/mar/assessment.asp?groupId=66302

5. Muhannad Al-Tarifi (Colorado University Associate Researcher, Jordanian citizen), personal interview with the author, February 6, 2014.

CHAPTER NOTES

6. Jordan, Refugees International. http://www.refugeesinternational.org/where-we-work/middle-east/jordan

7. Kristen Gillespie, "Jordan Faces Major Water Shortage." NPR News – Middle East, August 14, 2007. http://www.npr.org/templates/story/story.php?storyId=12768985

Chapter 5—Social Jordan

1. Matthew Teller, *The Rough Guide to Jordan* (London: Rough Guides, 2013), pp. 41, 48.

2. Sara Alamad (Colorado University student born and raised in Jordan), personal interview February 4, 2014.

3. Teller, *The Rough Guide*, p. 385.

4. Muhannad Al-Tarifi (Colorado Universtiy associate researcher, Jordanian citizen), personal interview with the author, February 6, 2014.

5 Alamad.

6. Al-Tarifi.

7. "Jordan," CIA World Factbook. https://www.cia.gov/library/publications/the-world-factbook/geos/jo.html

8. "The Amman Message," His Majesty King Abdullah II Ibn Al Hussein. http://kingabdullah.jo/index.php/en_US/initiatives/view/id/1.html

Chapter 6—Past Meets Present in the Arts

1. "Culture and Religion," The Embassy of the Hashemite Kingdom of Jordan. http://jordanembassyus.org/page/culture-and-religion

2. Ibid.

3. *Living Cultures—The Last Bedu of Petra and Wadi Rum (Jordan)*, (ZED. ADEQUAT Limited) http://www.youtube.com/watch?v=hhz2nTu-PFA

4. Fadia Faqir, "As soon as the fresh air touched my hair I began to cry." *The Guardian*, October 21, 2007. http://www.theguardian.com/world/2007/oct/22/religion.familyandrelationships

5. "Uncle Khalfan's Sheep," Al Salwa Books. http://alsalwabooks.com/page/View_Products.aspx?pid=84

6. Why Not?" Al Salwa Books. http://alsalwabooks.com/page/View_Products.aspx?pid=83

Chapter 7—Ancient Land, Modern Attitude

1. "Jordan: Magical Mystical Tour," Jordan Tourism Board North America. http://na2.visitjordan.com/Default.aspx?Tabid=755

2. Sara Alamad (Colorado University student born and raised in Jordan), personal interview February 4, 2014.

3. Jérôme, Raynaud. Living Cultures – The Last Bedu of Petra and Wadi Rum (Jordan). ZED. ADEQUAT Limited. http://www.youtube.com/watch?v=hhz2nTu-PFA

4. Jordan 2012 OSAC Crime and Safety Report, US Department of State Bureau of Diplomatic Security. https://www.osac.gov/pages/contentreportdetails.aspx?cid=12115

5. "Spread the Word," Queen Rania al Abdullah. http://www.queenrania.jo/education/global-education/spread-word

6. "The Economy," The Embassy of the Hashemite Kingdom of Jordan. http://jordanembassyus.org/page/economy

7. "Jordan," CIA World Factbook. https://www.cia.gov/library/publications/the-world-factbook/geos/jo.html

FURTHER READING

Books

Carew-Miller, Anna. *Jordan.* Broomall, PA: Mason Crest, 2004.

Englar, Mary. *Queen Rania of Jordan.* Mankato, MN: Capstone Press, 2009.

Kummer, Patricia K. *Jordan.* New York: Children's Press, 2007.

Romano, Amy. *Historical Atlas of Jordan.* New York: Rosen, 2003.

Skinner, Patricia. *Countries of the World—Jordan.* Milwaukee, WI: Gareth Stevens, 2003.

South, Coleman. *Cultures of the World—Jordan.* Tarrytown, NY: Marshall Cavendish Benchmark, 2007.

Works Consulted

1970: Civil War breaks out in Jordan, BBC News. http://news.bbc.co.uk/onthisday/hi/dates/stories/september/17/newsid_4575000/4575159.stm

Al Salwa Books
http://www.alsalwabooks.com/

Amos, Deborah and Nabih Bulos. "In A Rough Neighborhood, Jordan Clings To Its Stability." NPR—*Parallels*, July 1, 2013 (accessed February 12, 2014). http://www.npr.org/blogs/parallels/2013/07/01/196656296/stability-or-democracy-in-jordan-its-a-fragile-balance

Assessment for Palestinians in Jordan, Minorities at Risk. http://www.cidcm.umd.edu/mar/assessment.asp?groupId=66302

Cavendish, Richard. "Jordan Formally Annexes the West Bank." *History Today*, April 2000.

The Embassy of the Hashemite Kingdom of Jordan
http://jordanembassyus.org/

"Expressions of Identity: The Best Contemporary Jordanian Writers." The Culture Trip: Jordan, http://theculturetrip.com/middle-east/jordan/articles/expressions-of-identity-the-best-contemporary-jordanian-writers/

Gillespie, Kristen. "Jordan Faces Major Water Shortage." NPR News—Middle East, August 14, 2007. http://www.npr.org/templates/story/story.php?storyId=12768985

Haberman, Clyde. "Israel and Jordan Sign Peace Accord." *The New York Times*, October 26, 1994. https://www.nytimes.com/learning/general/onthisday/big/1026.html#article

Hashemite Kingdom of Jordan
http://www.kinghussein.gov.jo/office.html

His Majesty King Abdullah II Ibn Al Hussein
http://kingabdullah.jo/

"Jordan." The CIA World Factbook.
https://www.cia.gov/library/publications/the-world-factbook/geos/le.html

Jordan 2012 OSAC Crime and Safety Report. US Department of State Bureau of Diplomatic Security. https://www.osac.gov/pages/contentreportdetails.aspx?cid=12115

Jordan, Refugees International.
http://www.refugeesinternational.org/where-we-work/middle-east/jordan

FURTHER READING

The Jordan Tourism Board North America
   http://na2.visitjordan.com/

Jordan Visitor's Guide. Amman: Jordan Tourism Board, 2013. http://www.
   visitjordan.com/e_book/visitors_49-56.pdf

"King Abdullah: Jordan Needs 'Stable Middle Class.'" NPR News – Middle East,
   September 22, 2011. http://www.npr.org/2011/09/22/140670554/king-
   abdullah-jordan-needs-stable-middle-class

Metz, Helen Chapin (Editor). *Jordan: A Country Study.* Washington, DC: GPO
   for the Library of Congress, 1989.

Queen Rania al Abdullah
   http://www.queenrania.jo/

The Royal Society for the Conservation of Nature
   http://www.rscn.org.jo/

Su, Alice. "Syrian refugees adapt to Jordan legal system." Aljazeera, February 24,
   2014.http://www.aljazeera.com/indepth/features/2014/02/syrian-refugees-
   adapt-jordan-legal-system-20142247564334354.html

Teller, Matthew. *The Rough Guide to Jordan.* London: Rough Guides, 2013.

UNHCR—The UN Refugee Agency: 2014 UNHCR country operations profile—
   Jordan. http://www.unhcr.org/pages/4a02db416.html

United Nations Relief and Works Agency (accessed February 10, 2014)
   http://www.unrwa.org/

Walker, Jenny, and Matthew Firestone. *Lonely Planet: Jordan.* 7th Edition.
   Oakland, CA: Lonely Planet, 2009.

Documentaries

The 14 Wonders of the World—Ancient & New. Narrated by Pierce Brosnan.
   Chicago: Questar, 2008. DVD.

Al-Jamal, Mona, executive producer. *Wild Jordan.* Narrated by Chris Johnson.
   Royal Society for the Conservation of Nature. http://www.rscn.org.jo/orgsite/
   RSCN/Video/tabid/197/Default.aspx

Balit, Norbert, producer. *I Have Seen the Earth Change—Jordan.* An ADAMIS
   Production, 2010. http://www.youtube.com/watch?v=8QVuZ0TSoPE

Destination The Middle East. Ian Wright, narrator/traveller. Pilot Film
   Productions. Escapi, 2003. DVD.

Jordan: An Incentive Experience. Jordan Tourism Board. http://na2.visitjordan.
   com/Default.aspx?Tabid=755

Raynaud, Jérôme. *Living Cultures—The Last Bedu of Petra and Wadi Rum
   (Jordan).* ZED. ADEQUAT Limited. http://www.youtube.com/
   watch?v=hhz2nTu-PFA

Personal Interviews

Alamad, Sara (Colorado University student born and raised in Jordan).
   Personal interview with the author. February 4, 2014.

Al-Tarifi, Muhannad (Colorado University associate researcher, Jordanian
   citizen). Personal interview with the author. February 6, 2014.

GLOSSARY

Arabs (AIR-uhbs)—Descendants of people from the Arabian Peninsula.

armistice (ARM-uh-stuss)—Agreement to stop fighting.

colonnades (CAHL-uhn-ades)—Rows of columns that support a roof.

constitutional monarchy (cahn-stih-TOO-shuhn-uhl MAHN-ahr-chee)—A government in which a king or queen is the leader, with a legislature that makes and passes laws.

dabke (DAHB-kay)—A traditional folk dance.

domesticate (doh-MESS-tuh-cate)—Tame animals and breed them.

Eid al-Fitr (EED ahl-FIH-tur)—A three-day festival marking the end of Ramadan.

extremist (ehks-TREE-must)—Supporting actions or ideas far from what is considered normal.

hijab (hi-JAB)—A traditional covering for the hair and neck that many Muslim women wear.

Islam (ISS-lahm)—The religion of Muslims who follow the teachings of Muhammad.

jameed (jah-MEED)—Dried, salted yogurt made of goat's milk.

kaffiyeh (kah-FEE-yay)—A traditional headdress of Arab men.

mansaf (MAHN-saf)—The national dish in Jordan, made of yellow rice, lamb, jameed and roasted almonds.

mosaic (moh-ZAY-ik)—The art of creating a picture or pattern using small bits of glass, stone, or other materials.

mujadarra (moo-JAD-era)—A lentil and rice dish topped with cooked onions.

Muslim (MOOZ-lim)—A follower of Islam.

nomadic (noh-MAD-ik)—Moving from place to place without a permanent home.

oppression (oh-PRESH-uhn)—Cruel or unjust rule.

patriarchal (PAY-tree-ahr-kuhl)—A system led or controlled by males.

privatize (PRY-vuh-tize)—To sell a publically owned business to a private person or group.

progressive (pro-GRESS-ihv)—Favoring new, modern ideas or reform.

Qur'an (kuh-RAHN)—The Muslim holy book, said to contain the word of God.

Ramadan (RAHM-uh-dahn)—Muslim holy month of fasting and spiritual cleansing.

wadi (WAH-dee)—A canyon.

zaffeh (ZA-fay)—A procession of dancers and musicians that escorts a bride and groom to their wedding party.

za'tar (ZA-tar)—A blend of spices used in cooking.

Zionism (ZIE-uhn-izm)—The movement to establish a homeland for Jews in Palestine.

INDEX

About the Author

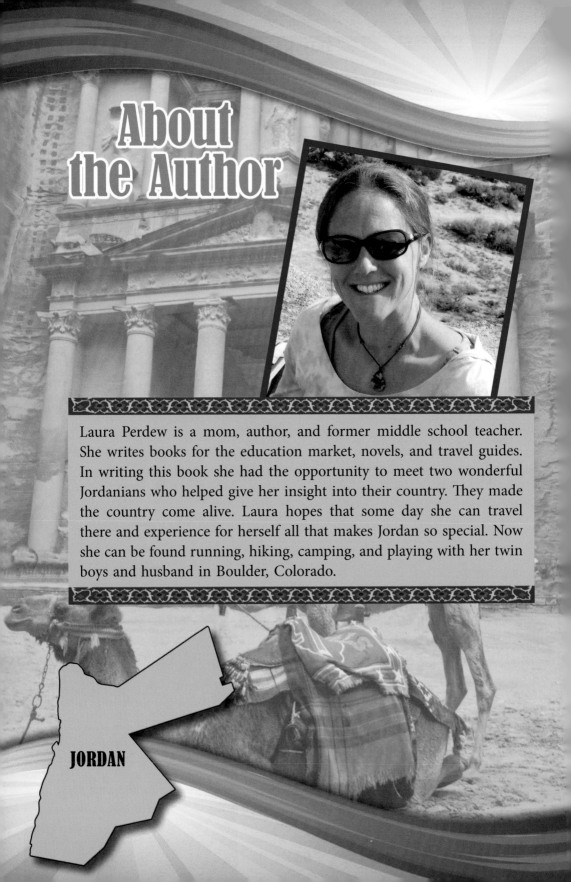

Laura Perdew is a mom, author, and former middle school teacher. She writes books for the education market, novels, and travel guides. In writing this book she had the opportunity to meet two wonderful Jordanians who helped give her insight into their country. They made the country come alive. Laura hopes that some day she can travel there and experience for herself all that makes Jordan so special. Now she can be found running, hiking, camping, and playing with her twin boys and husband in Boulder, Colorado.

JORDAN